Wiley

2018 CPAexcel®

EXAM REVIEW

FOCUS NOTES

Wiley

2018

CPAexcel®
EXAM REVIEW
FOCUS NOTES

BUSINESS ENVIRONMENT AND CONCEPTS

WILEY

Cover Design: Wiley
Cover image: © jeremykramerdesign/iStockphoto

For general information on our other products and services, or technical support, please contact our Customer Care Department within the United States at 800-762-2974, outside the United States at 317-572-3993 or fax 317-572-4002.

Wiley also publishes its books in a variety of electronic formats. Some content that appears in print may not be available in electronic books. For more information about Wiley products, visit our Web site at http://www.wiley.com.

ISBN: 978-1-119-48100-3 (paperback); 978-1-119-48098-3 (ebk); 978-1-119-48097-6 (ebk)

Printed in the United States of America
10 9 8 7 6 5 4 3 2 1

CONTENTS

Contents

Contents

Contents **viii**

PREFACE

This publication is a comprehensive yet simplified study program. It provides a review of all the basic skills and concepts tested on the CPA exam, and teaches important strategies to take the exam faster and more accurately. This tool allows you to take control of the CPA exam.

This simplified and focused approach to studying for the CPA exam can be used:

- As a handy and convenient reference manual
- To solve exam questions
- To reinforce material being studied

Included is all of the information necessary to obtain a passing score on the CPA exam in a concise and easy-to-use format. Due to the wide variety of information covered on the exam, a number of techniques are included:

- Acronyms and mnemonics to help you learn and remember a variety of rules and checklists
- Formulas and equations that simplify complex calculations required on the exam
- Simplified outlines of key concepts without the details that encumber or distract from learning the essential elements

- Techniques that can be applied to problem solving or essay writing, such as preparing a multiple-step income statement, determining who will prevail in a legal conflict, or developing an audit program
- Pro forma statements, reports, and schedules that make it easy to prepare these items by simply filling in the blanks
- Proven techniques to help you become a smarter, sharper, and more accurate test taker

This publication may also be useful to university students enrolled in Intermediate, Advanced, and Cost Accounting classes; Auditing, Business Law, and Federal Income Tax classes; or Economics and Finance classes.

CORPORATE GOVERNANCE
AND INTERNAL CONTROL

Corporate Rights, Responsibilities, and Authority

Corporate Governance: Establish Incentives and Monitoring

- Owners separate from management
- Agency problem: Will managers act in owners' interest?

Incentives to Defeat Agency Problem

Forms of Executive Compensation

- Base salary and profit: Usually based on accounting measures

    - May lead to earnings manipulation or taking excessive risk

---

Incentives to Defeat Agency Problem (continued)

- Stock options: align shareholders' and managers' interest in increasing share prices
  - Differences in timing horizons (management short term?)
  - Underwater options provide no incentive
- Restricted stock: force managers to think long term

Monitoring Devices

- Boards of directors
  - Independent nominating/corporate governance committee
  - Independent audit committee (AC) under Sarbanes-Oxley (SOX)
    - At least one financial expert
    - External auditors must report directly to AC
    - AC appoints, determines compensation, and oversees external auditor

Incentives to Defeat Agency Problem (continued)

- Stock exchange rules
  - Majority independent directors
    - Provide information to investors as to who is independent
  - Have and make available code of conduct
  - Have an independent AC (required by SOX)
  - Have an independent compensation committee (required by Dodd-Frank)
  - Clawback rules that require executives to pay back incentive compensation when there is an accounting restatement (required by Dodd-Frank)
  - Nonbinding shareholder votes on executive compensation and golden parachutes (required by Dodd-Frank)

Incentives to Defeat Agency Problem (continued)

- Internal auditors

  - Provide assurance on risk management and internal control
  - Should report at least indirectly to AC

    - Independent and competent
    - Chief IC officer reports directly to CEO
    - Should adhere to Institute of Internal Auditors (IIA) professional and ethical standards. These standards apply to both individual auditors and internal audit departments.

- External auditors

  - Help assure users that financials are accurate and not fraudulent
  - Must attest to management's assessment of effective internal control as required by SOX
  - The Jumpstart Our Business Startups (JOBS) Act exempted "emerging growth companies" for a maximum of five years from the date of their initial public offering from certain requirements that apply to larger public companies, including external reporting on internal control

Incentives to Defeat Agency Problem (continued)

- SEC and SOX

  - CEO and CFO must certify accuracy and truthfulness with criminal penalties
  - Fraud in sale or purchase of securities punishable by fine and/or prison
  - Destruction or other damage to documentation to hinder investigation punishable by fine and/or prison
  - Retaliation on "whistleblowers" punishable by fine and/or prison

17 Principles of Internal Control

Internal Controls

COSO: Internal Control Integrated Framework (Revised 2013)

Internal control is defined by COSO as a process, effected by the entity's board of directors, management, and other personnel, designed to provide reasonable assurance regarding the achievement of objectives relating to operations, reporting, and compliance. It has five components and 17 principles.

1. The **control environment** is the set of standards, processes, and structures that provide the basis for carrying out internal control across the organization. Principles include:

   a. Commitment to integrity and ethical values.
   b. The board of directors demonstrates independence from management and exercises oversight.
   c. Management establishes structures, reporting lines, and appropriate authorities and responsibilities in the pursuit of objectives.
   d. Commitment to attract, develop and retain competent individuals.
   e. Hold individuals accountable for their internal control responsibilities.

Internal Controls (continued)

2. **Risk assessment** is management's process for identifying, analyzing, and responding to risks. Principles include:

   a. Specify objectives with sufficient clarity to enable the identification and assessment of risks.

   b. Identify risks to the achievement of its objectives and analyze risks as a basis for determining how the risks should be managed.

   c. Consider the potential for fraud.

   d. Identify and assesses changes that could significantly impact internal control.

3. **Control activities** are policies and procedures that help ensure that management directives are carried out. Principles include:

   a. Select and develop control activities that contribute to the mitigation of risks.

   b. Select and develop general control activities over technology to support the achievement of objectives.

   c. Deploy control activities through policies that establish what is expected and in procedures that put policies into action.

Internal Controls (continued)

Control activities to mitigate risks include:

a. Authorizations and approvals

b. Verifications

c. Physical controls

d. Controls over standing data

e. Reconciliations

f. Supervisory controls

Internal Controls (continued)

4. The **information and communication** component of internal control supports all of the other components. Principles include:

    a. The organization obtains or generates and uses relevant, quality information to support the functioning of internal control.

    b. The organization internally communicates information, including objectives and responsibilities for internal control.

    c. The organization communicates with external parties regarding matters affecting the functioning of internal control.

5. **Monitoring activities** assess whether each of the five components is present and functioning. Principles include:

    a. Select, develop, and perform ongoing and/or separate evaluations to ascertain whether the components of internal control are present and functioning.

    b. Evaluate and communicate internal control deficiencies in a timely manner to those parties responsible for taking corrective action.

The COSO ERM Model

Enterprise Risk Management: Eight Components

1. Internal environment (tone of the organization)

   a. Effective board
   b. Ethical management
   c. Risk appetite: How much risk is organization willing to accept to achieve a goal?
   d. Risk tolerance: How far above or below meeting objective is allowable?

2. Objective setting

   a. Well-defined mission
   b. Process to set objectives that align with goals

3. Event identification

   a. Internal

      1) Loss of key personnel
      2) Damage to infrastructure (e.g., IS crash)
      3) Key product/process becomes obsolete

Enterprise Risk Management: Eight Components (continued)

      b.   External

            1)   Establish "trigger points" (e.g., competition increases market share above x amount)

            2)   Process to assess demographic and economic changes

      c.   Black swan analysis: Evaluate negative events that were unforeseen to determine why

4.   Risk assessment: What are the risks?

      a.   Assess impact and probability

      b.   Inherent risk: What if management does nothing in response to identified risk?

      c.   Residual risk: residual after management's response

Enterprise Risk Management: Eight Components (continued)

5. Risk responses

    a. Avoidance
    b. Reduction
    c. Sharing
    d. Acceptance

6. Control activities: Policies and procedures to insure that risk responses are implemented
7. Information and communication throughout organization

    a. Organization's objectives
    b. Risk appetite and tolerance
    c. Role of ERM in managing risk

8. Monitoring: Effective process to oversee ERM

Enterprise Risk Management: Limitations

1. The future is uncertain
2. No absolute assurances

    a. Human failure
    b. System breakdown
    c. Collusion across ERM
    d. Management override

INFORMATION TECHNOLOGY AND COMMUNICATIONS

Risks and Controls in Computer-Based Accounting Information

Consistency—Computers process data the same way every time.

Timeliness—Electronic processing and updating is normally more efficient.

Analysis—Data can be accessed for analytical procedures more conveniently (with proper software).

Monitoring—Electronic controls can be monitored by the computer system itself.

Circumvention—Controls are difficult to circumvent when programmed properly, and exceptions are unlikely to be permitted.

Risks and Controls in Computer-Based Accounting Information (continued)

Overreliance—Without clear output, IT systems are often assumed to be working when they are not.

Access—Destruction and alteration of large amounts of data are possible if unauthorized access occurs.

Changes in programs—Severe consequences without detection are possible if unauthorized program changes occur.

Failure to change—Programs are sometimes not updated for new laws, rules, or activities.

Manual intervention—Knowledgeable individuals can sometimes alter files by bypassing the appropriate programs.

Loss of data—Catastrophic data loss is possible if appropriate controls aren't in place.

The COBIT Model of IT Governance and Management

COBIT 5 is a framework for integrating IT with business strategy and governance. It incorporates the following five principles:

1. Meeting stakeholder needs
2. Covering the enterprise end-to-end
3. Applying a single integrated framework
4. Enabling a holistic approach
5. Separating governance from management

The COBIT Model of IT Governance and Management (continued)

COBIT 5 enablers include:
- Processes—an organized set of practices to achieve objectives
- Organizational structures—the key decision-making entities in an organization
- Culture, ethics, and behavior of individuals and the organization
- Principles, policies and frameworks
- Information produced and used by the enterprise
- Services, infrastructure, and applications
- People, skills, and competencies required for successful completion of activities and making accurate decisions

Organizational Continuity Planning and Disaster Recovery

Unanticipated interruptions are avoided through **contingency planning** that includes fault-tolerant systems and backup files. One approach to backup is the **grandfather-parent-child** procedure in which three generations of files are retained.

A contingency plan will include a **disaster recovery plan** to prepare for the possibility of fires, floods, earthquakes, or terrorist bombings. The plan should specify backup sites to be used for alternate processing.

- A **hot site** is a location that includes a computer system that is already configured similarly to the system regularly used by the company, allowing for immediate use.
- A **cold site** is a location where power and space are available allowing for the installation of processing equipment on short notice.

Controls over **computer facilities** should include locating the facility in a safe place, limiting access to appropriate employees, and maintaining insurance.

Passwords or other forms of identification should be used to limit **access to computer files**.

System Development and Implementation

A Seven-Step Process (PADDTIM)

1. **P**lanning
   a. Define system to be developed
   b. Determine project scope
   c. Develop project plan
2. **A**nalysis
   a. Meet with users and IS staff
   b. Conduct needs assessment of users
   c. Conduct gap analysis between needs and existing systems
3. **D**esign (technical blueprint of new system)
4. **D**evelopment: Build
   a. Platform
   b. Software

A Seven-Step Process (PADDTIM) (continued)

5. Testing
   a. Unit tests (pieces of code)
   b. System tests (Do units within a system integrate?)
   c. Integration testing (Do separate systems integrate?)
   d. User acceptance
6. Implementation: several strategies
   a. Parallel implementation: run old and new
   b. Plunge: Stop old, use new
   c. Pilot
   d. Phased
7. Maintenance
   a. Monitor and support
      1) Training
      2) Help desk
      3) Process and policies for authorizing changes

Introduction to E-Business and E-Commerce

Electronic commerce using **electronic data interchange** or **EDI** adds to the complexity of auditing. EDI enables:

- Communication without the use of paper
- Electronic funds transfers and sales over the Internet
- Simplification of the recording process using scanning devices
- Sending information to trading partners as transactions occur

EDI transactions are formatted using strict standards that have been agreed to worldwide, often requiring companies to acquire translation software.

Risks of E-Commerce

Electronic commerce increases the risk of improper use of information. Controls might include:

- Data encryption
- Controls to prevent electronic eavesdropping

There is also the risk of improper distribution of transactions with information being electronically transmitted to an inappropriate company. Controls might include:

- Routing verification procedures
- Message acknowledgement procedures

The reduction in the paper audit trail associated with EDI creates special challenges to the auditor.

- Detection risk may not be sufficiently reduced through substantive testing
- Control risk must be reduced adequately to achieve an acceptable level of audit risk
- Controls must be built into the system to insure the validity of information captured

Data Structures, Software, and Databases

Bit—A single switch in a computer that is either in the on (1) or off (0) position

Byte—A group of eight bits representing a character

Character—A letter, number, punctuation mark, or special character

Alphanumeric—A character that is either a letter or number

Field—A group of related characters representing a unit of information (such as a phone number or a city name)

Record—A group of logically related fields (such as the name, address, and telephone of one employee)

File—A group of logically related records (such as the contact information for all the employees)

- Master file—A permanent source that is used as an ongoing reference and that is periodically updated
- Detail file—A file listing a group of transactions that can be used to update a master file

Data Structures, Software, and Databases (continued)

Software is either system software or application software.

- **System software** is made up of the programs that run the system and direct its operations. It is comprised of the operating system and utility programs
- **Utility** programs are used for sorts, merges, and other routine functions to maintain and improve the efficiency of a computer system
- **Communication software** handles transmission of data between different computers
- Specialized **security software** is a type of utility program used to control access to the computer or its files

Programming languages:

- **Source program** is in the language written by the programmer (high-level languages resemble English while assembly languages are closer to direct machine instructions)
- **Object program** is in a form the machine understands (on-off or 1-0)
- **Compiler** is a program that converts source programs into machine language

Information Systems Hardware

Hardware is the actual electronic equipment. Common components include:

- **Central processing unit** or **CPU**—The principal hardware component that processes programs
- **Memory**—The internal storage space or **online storage**, often referred to as **random access memory** or **RAM**
- **Offline storage**—Devices used to store data or programs externally, including floppy disks, magnetic tape, digital video discs (DVDs), and compact discs (CDs)
- **File server**—A computer with a large internal memory used to store programs and data that can be accessed by all workstations in the network
- **Input and output devices**—Devices that allow for communication between the computer and users and for the storage of data, such as a terminal with a screen and a keyboard, scanners, microphones, wireless handheld units, barcode readers, point-of-sale registers, optical character readers, mark sense readers, light guns, printers, speakers, CD and DVD drives, magnetic tape drives, and magnetic disk drives

Size and Power of Computers

Hardware comes in various sizes, depending on the volume and complexity of users' needs. In declining order of power, computer hardware includes:

- **Supercomputers**—Common for massive scale needs by science and math departments of universities and large governmental operations
- **Mainframe computers**—Until recently, often the only computer a large organization might have, with several terminals having the ability to connect to it simultaneously
- **Minicomputers**—Until recently, a less expensive alternative to mainframes used by smaller organizations as their primary computer with accessibility through multiple terminals
- **Microcomputers**—Personal computers designed for use by a single individual, including desktops and laptops
- **Personal digital assistants**—Handheld computers with limited processing capabilities that normally emphasize easy connection and transfer of data with the primary microcomputer used by an individual

Storage Devices

Magnetic tape—Inexpensive form of storage used primarily for backup, since only **sequential** access of data is possible.

Magnetic disks—Permanent storage devices inside a computer (including hard drives) that allow **random** access to data without the need to move forward or backward through all intervening data. Some systems use **RAID** (redundant array of independent disks), which includes multiple disks in one system so that data can be stored redundantly and the failure of one of the disks won't cause the loss of any data.

Removable disks—Transportable forms of storage. In increasing order of capacity, these include:

- Compact discs (CDs)
- Optical discs (DVDs)

Transaction Processing

The two primary approaches to the processing of data are batch processing and online processing.

1. **Batch processing**—Input data is collected over a period of time and processed periodically
2. **Online processing**—Individuals originating transactions process them from remote locations in a batch, similar to batch processing, or immediately in an **online**, **real-time system**

Online, real-time systems update accounting records immediately as transactions occur, but result in significant changes in internal control.

- Source documents are often not available to support input into the computer
- The audit trail is usually significantly reduced, requiring controls programmed into the computer

Computer Networks and Data Communications

In a computer network, computers are connected to one another to enable sharing of peripheral devices, sharing data and programs stored on a **file server**, and communicating with one another.

Networks allow various user departments to share information files maintained in **databases**. Databases should:

- Provide departments with information that is appropriate
- Prevent access to inappropriate information

A company may create its own **value-added network** or **VAN**.

- A **local area network** (**LAN**) is used when computers are physically near to one another
- A **wide area network** (**WAN**) uses high-speed, long-distance communications networks or satellites to connect computers that are not near to one another

Cloud computing is the use and access of multiple server-based computational resources via a digital network (WAN, Internet connection using the World Wide Web, etc.)

Computer Networks and Data Communications (continued)

To minimize control risk, a network should have some form of security that limits access to certain files to authorized individuals.

- Certain individuals may have read-only access to files
- Others will be authorized to alter the data in the files

A **virus** is a program that requests a computer to perform an activity that is not authorized by the user. A **worm** is a program that duplicates itself over a network so as to infect many computers with viruses.

A tool for establishing security is a **firewall**, which prevents unauthorized users from accessing data.

The Internet—Structure and Protocols

The **Internet** is a worldwide network that allows virtually any computer system to link to it by way of an electronic gateway. The Internet facilitates data communication services including:

- Remote login
- File transfer
- Electronic mail
- Newsgroups
- Videoconferencing
- Groupware systems

Intranets use Internet technology in closed networks.

Extranets use Internet technology to link businesses with suppliers, customers, and others.

Networks are part of a decentralized processing system applying **distributed data processing**. Users share programs, peripheral devices, and data.

In **client/server computing**, smaller programs are distributed to the workstations, enabling the user to communicate with the network. This is referred to as front-end processing.

In **end user computing**, a user department generates and uses its own information.

The Internet—Structure and Protocols (continued)

To make use of the Internet more user-friendly, a framework for accessing documents was developed, known as the World Wide Web

- **Hypertext Transfer Protocol (HTTP)**—The language commonly understood by different computers to communicate via the Internet
- **Document**—A single file on any computer that is accessible through the Internet
- **Page**—The display that results from connection to a particular document on the Internet
- **Uniform Resource Locator (URL)**—The "address" of a particular page on the Internet
- **Web browser**—A program that allows a computer with a particular form of operating software to access the Internet and that translates documents for proper display
- **Server**—The computer that is "sending" the pages for display on another computer
- **Client**—The computer that is "receiving" the pages and seeing the display
- **Upload**—Sending information from a client to a server computer
- **Download**—Sending information from a server to a client computer

The Internet—Structure and Protocols (continued)

Web 2.0 is a second generation of the web. Refers to era of web-based collaboration and community generated content via web-based software tools such as

- **Blog**—An asynchronous discussion, or web log, led by a moderator that typically focuses on a single topic
- **Wiki**—An information-gathering and knowledge-sharing website that is developed collaboratively by a community or group
- **Twitter**—A micro-variation of a blog. Restricts input (tweets) to 140 characters

Many companies use software to monitor and manage their reputations in social media.

ECONOMIC CONCEPTS

Demand

As the price of a product increases, the quantity demanded by buyers decreases. This is reflected by a demand curve that is plotted with quantity demands on the x-axis (horizontal) and price on the y-axis (vertical):

Demand Curve Shifts

When some variables other than the price of the product causes demand to change, it is referred to as a **demand curve shift.**

Positive shift—An increase in demand at each price (the line moves to the right)

Negative shift—A decrease in demand at each price (the line moves to the left)

This is an illustration of a positive demand curve shift:

Positive Demand Curve Shift

Certain factors have a **direct** relationship to the demand curve for a product (an increase in that factor will cause the demand curve to have a positive shift to the right):

- **The price of substitute goods**—When another product may be an acceptable alternative, an increase in its price will make the present product more attractive. For example, an increase in the price of hamburgers will cause a positive shift in the demand for hot dogs.
- **Expectations of price increases**—Consumers are more likely to buy now if they think prices will be going up in the future.
- **Consumer income and wealth**—For **normal goods**, the demand will increase if consumers have more wealth to spend on goods.
- **Size of the market**—When new consumers are available to purchase a product, such as when trade barriers between countries are removed, demand for the product will increase.

Negative Demand Curve Shift

Certain factors have an **inverse** relationship to the demand curve for a product (an increase in that factor will cause the demand curve to have a negative shift to the left):

- **The price of complementary goods**—When products are normally used together, an increase in the price of one of the goods harms demand for the other. For example, an increase in the price of hamburgers will cause a negative shift in the demand for hamburger buns.
- **Consumer income and wealth**—For **inferior goods**, the demand will decrease if consumers have more wealth to spend on goods. For example, the demand for tire patches will likely decrease as people become wealthier, since they are more likely to be able to replace the tires rather than patch them.
- **Group boycott**—An organized boycott will, if effective, decrease the demand for a product.

Other factors affect the demand curve in significant but indeterminate ways, such as changes in consumer tastes.

Supply

As the price of a product increases, the quantity offered by sellers increases. This is reflected by a supply curve that is plotted with quantity on the x-axis (horizontal) and price on the y-axis (vertical):

Supply Curve Shifts

When some variable other than the price of the product causes supply to change, it is referred to as a **supply curve shift.**

Positive shift—An increase in supply at each price (the line moves to the right)

Negative shift—A decrease in supply at each price (the line moves to the left)

This is an illustration of a positive supply curve shift:

Factors Causing a Supply Curve Shift

Factors with a **direct** relationship on the supply curve include:

- Number of producers
- Government subsidies
- Price expectations

Factors with an **inverse** relationship on the supply curve include:

- Changes in production costs
- Prices of other goods

Focus on
Economic Concepts

Market Equilibrium

The price at which the quantity demanded and quantity offered intersect is the equilibrium price:

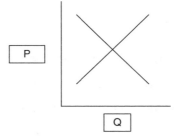

When the government intervenes to impose price ceilings, setting the price below equilibrium, the quantity demanded will exceed quantity offered, resulting in shortages of goods. When the government intervenes to impose price floors, setting price above equilibrium, the quantity offered will exceed quantity demanded, resulting in unsold surpluses of goods.

Elasticity

Price Elasticity = Percentage change in quantity demanded / Percentage change in price

If elasticity is greater than 1, demand is considered **elastic**, and total revenue will decline if the price is increased, since the percentage drop in demand exceeds the percentage increase in price. A firm will be unable to pass on cost increases to consumers in these circumstances.

If elasticity is equal to 1, demand is considered **unitary**, and total revenue will remain the same if the price is increased.

If elasticity is less than 1, demand is considered **inelastic**, and total revenue will increase if the price is increased, since the percentage increase in price exceeds the decrease in demand. A firm will be able to raise prices in these circumstances.

Income Elasticity = Percentage change in quantity demanded / Percentage change in income

This will be a positive number for normal goods and a negative number for inferior goods.

Cross-Elasticity = Percentage change in demand for product X / Percentage change in price of product Y

This will be a positive number for substitute goods and a negative number for complements.

Consumer Demand and Utility Theory

Marginal utility—The satisfaction value to consumers of the next dollar they spend on a particular product.

Law of diminishing marginal utility—The more a consumer has of a particular product, the less valuable will be the next unit of that product. As a result, a consumer maximizes satisfaction when the last dollar spent on each product generates the exact same amount of marginal utility.

Personal disposable income—The available income of a consumer after subtracting payment of taxes or adding receipt of government benefits. The consumer will either spend (consume) or save this income.

Marginal propensity to consume (MPC)—The percentage of the next dollar in personal disposable income that the consumer would be expected to spend.

Marginal propensity to save (MPS)—The percentage of the next dollar in personal disposable income that the consumer would be expected to save (MPC plus MPS must equal 100%, or 1).

Inputs and the Cost of Production

Short-Run Costs of Production

Over short periods of time and limited ranges of production, costs include **fixed** and **variable** components:

Fixed costs—Costs that won't change even when there is a change in production. Average fixed costs are total fixed costs divided by units produced. An example is rent paid on the production facility.

Variable costs—Costs that will rise as production rises. Average variable costs are total variable costs divided by units produced. An example is materials used in the manufacture of the product.

Total costs—The sum of fixed and variable costs. Average total costs are total costs divided by units produced.

Marginal cost—The increase in cost that will result from an increase in one unit in production. Only variable costs are relevant, since fixed costs won't increase in such circumstances.

Long-Run Costs of Production

In the long run, all costs are variable, since increasing production beyond certain levels will require increases in capacity, causing even "fixed" costs to rise.

Return to scale is the increase in units produced (output) that results from an increase in production costs (input).

Return to scale = Percentage increase in output / Percentage increase in input

When return to scale is greater than 1, we have **increasing returns to scale**. This will normally occur up to a certain level for all firms because of **economies of scale**, or the increased efficiency that results from producing more units of a product (such as the ability to have employees specialize in different tasks and improve their abilities).

When return to scale is less than 1, we have **decreasing returns to scale**. This will normally occur beyond a certain level for all firms because of **diseconomies of scale**, or the increased inefficiencies that result from expanding production (such as the greater difficulty management has in controlling the activities of larger numbers of employees and facilities).

Firms should not increase production beyond levels at which marginal revenue from output exceeds marginal costs from inputs.

Gross Measures—Economic Activity

Gross domestic product (GDP)—The price of all goods and services produced by a domestic economy for a year at current market prices.

Real GDP—GDP adjusted to remove the effect of price inflation in the goods and services. In theory, real GDP growth above a certain level (called **potential GDP**) results in price inflation.

Gross national product (GNP)—The price of all goods and services produced by labor and property supplied by the nation's residents. It differs from GDP in two ways:

1. GNP includes income received by the nation's resident from other countries for products that are a part of foreign economies.
2. GNP excludes payments made to the residents of other countries for products that are a part of the domestic economy.

GDP/GNP may be computed using one of two different approaches:

1. **Income approach**—National income plus depreciation (and a few small adjustments)
2. **Expenditure approach**—Consumption plus private investment plus government purchases (and a few small adjustments)

Gross Measures—Employment/Unemployment

The unemployment rate is the percentage of those people who are looking for work who are currently not employed. There are three types of unemployment:

1. **Frictional**—This represents the time period during which people are unemployed as a result of changing jobs or newly entering the workforce. Because of the mobility of society, there is always some level of this type of unemployment, even in a society that effectively has "full" employment.

2. **Structural**—This represents potential workers whose job skills do not match the needs of the workforce as a result of changing demand for goods and services of technological advances that reduce or eliminate the need for the skills they possess. Such unemployment normally requires retraining in order for these individuals to be employable again.

3. **Cyclical**—This represents the unemployment caused by variations in the business cycle, when real GDP fails to grow at the pace necessary to employ all willing workers.

Aggregate Demand and Supply

Effects of Price Inflation

Just as there are demand and supply curves for individual products, aggregate curves can be depicted for overall prices and production of goods and services of an entire economy. Price inflation will shift the aggregate demand curve for several reasons:

- **Interest rate effect**—Price inflation causes an increase in interest rates and decreases the willingness of consumers to borrow, causing a negative shift in the demand curve for items whose purchase is typically financed, such as houses and automobiles.
- **Wealth effect**—Price inflation causes the value of fixed income investments (such as bonds) to decrease, causing individuals to have less wealth and reducing their consumption of normal goods. (The consumption of inferior goods will increase, but these are typically a small part of the overall economy.)
- **International purchasing power effect**—Domestic price inflation makes domestic goods and services more expensive relative to foreign goods and services, causing an increased demand for foreign products and a negative shift in the demand curve for domestic goods and services.

Business Cycle

Expansion—Periods of increased aggregate spending will cause a positive shift in the demand curve to the right and result in a higher equilibrium GDP. Technological advances will cause a positive shift in the supply curve and also result in a higher equilibrium GDP.

Contraction—Periods of decreased aggregate spending will shift the demand curve to the left and result in a lower equilibrium GDP. Trade wars between nations (and wars in general) cause a negative shift in the supply curve and also cause a decline in GDP.

Recession—Two consecutive quarters of negative GDP growth.

Depression—A contraction of GDP that continues for a long period of time. (There is no formal agreement as to the length of time a recession must continue to be called a depression, but it will usually be multiple years.)

Panic—A severe contraction of GDP occurring within a very short time frame (generally lasting less than a year).

Recovery—The term used to refer to the period of expansion that follows the end of a contraction.

Indicators of Business Cycles

Leading indicator—A measure that is being used to try to predict recoveries and recessions. These indicators will normally start moving up months before an actual recovery begins and start moving down months before an actual recession beings. There are many such indicators with variable success in predicting the business cycle. One of the most useful is changes in **stock market prices**.

Coincident indicator—A measure that normally moves up and down simultaneously with economic recoveries and recessions, respectively, and is used to determine if the economy is expanding or contracting at the present time. One example is **industrial production**.

Lagging indicator—A measure that normally starts moving up months after a recovery has begun and starts declining months after a recession has begun. It is used to confirm evidence that the economy has been expanding or contracting over the past few months. A commonly used lagging indicator is the **average prime rate** for bank loans.

Price Levels and Inflation/Deflation

There are three common measures of price inflation:

1. **Consumer price index (CPI)**—This measures the price of a fixed basket of goods and services that a typical urban consumer might purchase in relation to the price of the same goods and services in an earlier base period.
2. **Producer price index (PPI)**—This measures a fixed basket of goods at the wholesale cost to dealers (such as retail stores) rather than the price to consumers.
3. **GDP deflator**—This utilizes the total production of the economy as measured by GDP and is used to convert GDP to real GDP.

A decline in general price levels is known as **deflation**.

Demand-Pull Inflation

When aggregate spending increases, the **demand** curve moves to the **right**, causing the market equilibrium to occur at higher price levels:

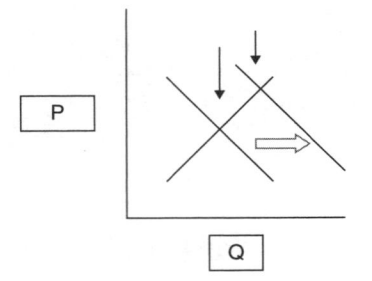

Notice that the equilibrium point occurs at a higher level of prices AND quantity. This is the basis for the historical theory that higher inflation results in higher productivity and, therefore, lower unemployment. The trade-off between inflation and unemployment is known as the **Phillips curve**. Many modern economists reject this theory, or believe that increases in inflation cause only a temporary decline in unemployment.

Cost-Push Inflation

When production costs increase, the **supply** curve moves to the **left**, causing the market equilibrium to occur at higher price levels:

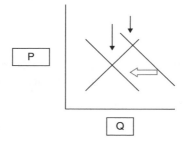

Notice that the equilibrium occurs at a higher level of prices but at a lower quantity. This means that prices are rising but output is declining, usually resulting in higher unemployment. This effect directly contradicts the theory of the Phillips curve.

Money, Banking, and Monetary/Fiscal Policy

There will be a positive shift in the demand curve when there is an increase in spending by consumers, businesses, or governments. The size of the shift will be significantly larger than the amount spent, due to the **multiplier effect** of increased spending increasing the income of suppliers, who in turn will spend more, increasing the income of other suppliers, and so on.

The size of the multiplier effect depends on the percentage of increased income that is expected to be spent, or the **marginal propensity to consume,** and the related percentage of increased income that is expected to be saved, or the **marginal propensity to save**. (These two must add up to 1 for the overall economy just as they did for each individual consumer.)

The increase in the equilibrium GDP that results from an injection of new spending is:

Change in spending / Marginal propensity to save

For example, if those making up the economy overall are likely to spend 75% of increased income and save the other 25%, then a change in spending of $100 will raise GDP by $400:

$$\$100 / 25\% = \$400$$

Money, Banking, and Monetary/Fiscal Policy (continued)

Fiscal policy—By the manner in which it collects taxes and spends, the government may try to aid certain industries or the economy as a whole. A common technique is known as **fiscal expansion** or **deficit spending**, which involves raising spending levels without an equivalent increase in taxes or lowering taxes without an equivalent decrease in spending. The goal is to increase aggregate spending in the economy and benefit from the multiplier effect.

Monetary policy—The Federal Reserve System (or "Fed") is charged with control over the money supply. By taking actions that increase (known as expansionary policies) or decrease (known as contractionary policies) the total amount of money in circulation, the Fed has a major impact on total spending. It has various techniques at its disposal:

- **Reserve requirements**—The Fed sets requirements on banks as to the percentage of checking deposit money received from customers that may not be loaned out.
- **Open-market operations**—The Fed can buy or sell government securities on the open market and thereby increase or decrease the money supply outstanding.
- **Discount rate**—The Fed can change the cost of money to banks and thereby cause a change in interest rates throughout the economy.

Focus on

Economic Concepts

Reasons for International Activity

Because of differences in resources, climate, and specific skills, countries that trade goods and services with each other normally raise the standard of living of the people in both nations. Each country will focus on its advantages:

- **Absolute advantage**—This exists when the country can produce the goods at a lower cost than the other country.
- **Comparative advantage**—This exists when the cost of producing those goods relative to the cost of producing other goods is lower in that country than in the other country.

Even if one country has an absolute advantage over the other with respect to all goods, there will be trade benefits to both from each focusing on its comparative advantage. (On an individual level, a skilled CPA who is able to type 80 words per minute would still benefit from having word processing performed by a secretary who can type only 40 words per minute and who has no accounting skills.)

Obstacles to Free Trade

Free trade is restricted by **tariffs** (taxes on the importing of goods) and quotas (limits on the quantity that may be imported). When restrictions are imposed, their **direct** effects are:

- *Domestic producers: Positive.* Their demand curve shifts to the right as the availability of substitute goods has been reduced. They sell more goods at higher prices. Usually the managements and unions of these producers sought the restrictions.
- *Domestic users: Negative.* Their supply curve is being shifted to the left. As a result, they end up paying higher prices and acquiring fewer goods overall.
- *Foreign producers: Negative.* Their demand curve shifts to the left because the number of potential buyers has been reduced. They sell fewer goods at lower prices.
- *Foreign users: Positive.* Their supply curve shifts to the right, as their producers will have to do more selling in their own market. They buy more goods at lower prices.

A crucial **indirect** effect of trade restrictions is retaliation by other countries. The **World Trade Organization (WTO)** was formed to encourage all countries to maintain free trade policies and to prevent trade wars. The **North American Free Trade Agreement (NAFTA)** was signed by the United States, Mexico, and Canada in order to remove trade restrictions existing between those countries.

Focus on
Economic Concepts

Balance of Payments

This is an account summary of the transactions of a nation with others.

Current account—The flow of goods and services and government transfers during a specific period of time:

- **Balance of trade**—The difference between the goods exported and good imported. If exports are higher, then a trade surplus exists; if imports are higher, a deficit exists.
- **Balance of goods and services**—The same comparison, but with services included

Capital account—The flow of investments in fixed and financial assets

Balance of payments—The combined surplus or deficit from the current and capital accounts

Official reserve account—The total of gold and foreign currency held by the nation

Currency Exchange Rate Issue

The value of the currencies of different nations will fluctuate relative to one another based on the supply and demand for these currencies. Exchange rates between currencies include:

- **Spot rate**—The exchange rate for currencies that will be immediately delivered
- **Forward rate**—The rate at which two parties agree they will exchange the currencies at a specific future date (called the settlement date)

Forward rates differ from spot rates based on expectations that the relative values of the two currencies will change between now and then. Factors affecting foreign exchange rates:

- **Inflation**—The currency with higher inflation will fall in value relative to the other.
- **Interest rates**—The currency in the nation with higher interest rates will rise in value.
- **Balance of payments**—The currency of the country that is a net exporter will rise in value.
- **Government intervention**—The currency will rise if official reserves are used to buy it.
- **Political and economic stability**—The currency will fall when there are threats to stability.

Introduction to Business Strategy and Market Analysis

Strategic planning involves identifying an organization's long-term goals and determining the best approaches to achieving those goals.

- Develop mission
- Develop vision
- Perform situational analysis to identify internal and external forces that may affect the organization's performance and choice of strategies and assess the organization's strengths, weaknesses, opportunities, and threats (a SWOT analysis)

Generic Strategies

- Product differentiation
- Cost leadership

FINANCIAL MANAGEMENT

Introduction to Financial Management

Five functions:

1. **Financing**—Raising capital to fund the business
2. **Capital budgeting**—Selecting the best long-term projects based on risk and return
3. **Financial management**—Managing cash flow so that funds are available when needed at the lowest cost
4. **Corporate governance**—Ensuring behavior by managers that is ethical and in the best interests of shareholders
5. **Risk management**—Identifying and managing the firm's exposure to all types of risk

Leverage

Operating leverage—The degree to which a firm has built fixed costs into its operations

- Higher fixed costs mean more risk when revenues are below expectations
- Profit grows rapidly relative to revenue increases due to lower variable costs
- % change in operating income / % change in unit volume = Degree of operating leverage

Financial leverage—The degree to which a firm uses debt financing in its business

- Higher debt means higher interest and principal obligations for repayment, increasing risk if performance is not up to expectations
- Debt financing costs less than equity financing and doesn't increase with greater performance, so overall profit and asset growth potential is greater
- % change in earnings per share / % change in earnings before interest and taxes = Degree of financial leverage

Cost Concepts

Debt—The cost of debt financing is the after-tax cost of interest payments, as measured by the yield to maturity. It can be calculated in two ways:

1. Yield to maturity $\times$ (1 − Effective tax rate)
2. (Interest expense − Tax deduction for interest) / Carrying value of debt

Preferred stock—The cost of preferred stock financing is the stipulated dividend divided by the issue price of the stock.

Common stock—The cost of common stock financing represents the expected returns of the common shareholders and is difficult to estimate. Some techniques:

- **Capital asset pricing model (CAPM)**—Volatility of stock price relative to average stock. This model assumes the expected return of a particular stock depends on its volatility (beta) relative to the overall stock market. CAPM = Beta $\times$ Excess of normal market return over risk-free investments + Normal return on risk-free investments
- **Arbitrage pricing model**—This model is a more sophisticated CAPM with separate excess returns and betas for each component making up the stock characteristics

Cost Concepts *(continued)*

- **Bond yield plus**—This uses the normal historical relationship between equities and debt and simply adds 3% to 5% to the interest rate on the firm's long-term debt
- **Dividend yield plus growth rate**—This takes the current dividend as a percentage of the stock price and adds the expected growth rate in earnings

Weighted-average cost of capital—This is a calculation of a firm's effective cost of capital, taking into account the portion of its capital that was obtained by debt, preferred stock, and common stock. For example, if 40% of capital was obtained through long-term debt at an effective cost of 6%, 10% of capital was obtained by issuing preferred stock with an effective cost of 8%, and 50% of capital was obtained by issuing common stock expected to return 11% to shareholders, the weighted-average cost of capital is:

$$40\% \times 6\% + 10\% \times 8\% + 50\% \times 11\%$$

$$= 2.4\% + 0.8\% + 5.5\%$$

$$= 8.7\%$$

Time Value of Money Tools

Many decisions require adjustments related to the time value of money:

- **Present value of amount**—This is used to examine a single cash flow that will occur at a future date and determine its equivalent value today.
- **Present value of ordinary annuity**—This refers to repeated cash flows on a systematic basis, with amounts being paid at the end of each period. (It may also be known as an annuity in arrears.) Bond interest payments are commonly made at the end of each period and use these factors.
- **Present value of annuity due**—This refers to repeated cash flows on a systematic basis, with amounts being paid at the beginning of each period. (It may also be known as an annuity in advance or special annuity.) Rent payments are commonly made at the beginning of each period and use these factors.
- **Future values**—These look at cash flows and project them to some future date, and include all three variations applicable to present values.
- **Interest rates**—Usually, two components:
  1. Expected inflation/deflation rates
  2. Inflation-adjusted return for the investment (risk adjusted)

Interest Rate Concepts and Calculations

This term refers to the price that borrowers must pay for the use of money.

- **Nominal interest rate**—The rate as measured in terms of the nation's currency
- **Real interest rate**—The rate adjusted for inflation
- **Risk-free interest rate**—The rate that would be charged to a borrower if the lender had an absolute certainty of being repaid (The rate paid on United States Treasury securities is often considered to be a useful measure of the risk-free interest rate.)
- **Discount rate**—The rate set by the Federal Reserve System at which a bank can borrow from a Federal Reserve bank
- **Prime rate**—The rate that banks charge their most creditworthy customers on short-term loans from the bank

Financial Valuation

Three major valuation models for financial instruments assets in order of reliability:

1. Market values from active markets for identical assets
   a. Assumes sufficient volume
2. Active markets for similar assets
   a. Must adjust for differences in instruments, for example:
      1) Block sales
      2) Credit risks
      3) Maturity/exercise dates
3. Valuation models
   a. In absence of active markets, assume hypothetical seller/buyer
   b. Generally use discounted cash flow
   c. Must use assumptions that are reasonable and consistent with existing general market information

Introduction and the Payback Period Approach

Used to evaluate capital expenditures—uses two equations

      Cash inflows before tax
-   Depreciation on investment
=   Increase in taxable income
-   Tax
=   Increase in accounting net income

	Cash inflows before tax	**or**		Increase in accounting net income
−	Tax		+	Depreciation on investment
=	After-tax net cash inflows		=	After-tax net cash inflows

Payback Method

        Initial investment
÷   After tax net cash inflows
=   Payback period

Payback period is compared to target period

- If shorter, investment is acceptable
- If longer, investment is unacceptable

Traditional payback method does not take into account time value of money

Present value payback method considers the time value of money

Accounting Rate of Return Approach

Increase in accounting net income

÷   Investment

=   Accounting rate of return

Investment may be

- Initial investment
- Long-term average – (Initial investment + Salvage value) / 2
- Short-term average – (Beginning carrying value + Ending carrying value) / 2

Return compared to target rate

- If greater, investment is acceptable
- If lower, investment is unacceptable

Accounting rate of return does not consider the time value of money

Net Present Value Approach

         After-tax net cash inflows
$\times$ Present value factor for annuity at target rate
$=$ Present value of investment
$-$ Initial investment
$=$ Net present value

If positive, investment is acceptable—if negative, investment is unacceptable

Internal Rate of Return Approach

	Initial investment
÷	After tax net cash inflows
=	Present value factor (same as payback period)

Present value factor is compared to factors for same # of periods (life of investment) to determine effective interest rate

- Factor may be equal to amount at specific interest rate
- If factor falls between amounts, rate is estimated

Resulting rate compared to target rate

- If greater, investment is acceptable
- If lower, investment is unacceptable

Introduction and Financial/Capital Structure

Long-Term Debt

Private debt—Loans obtained from banks and other financial institutions or from syndicates of lenders. Virtually all such loans have variable interest rates that are tied to an index:

- **Prime rate**—This is the rate that the lender charges its most creditworthy customers. Loans to other customers would include a fixed amount above this (e.g., prime plus 2%).
- **London Interbank Offered Rate (LIBOR)**—When the borrower and lender are in different countries, the base used will typically be the LIBOR rather than the prime rate.

Public debt—To bypass institutional lenders, a corporation may sell bonds directly to investors as a means of borrowing, with fixed interest rates and maturity dates for the securities, which can then trade on the open market.

- **SEC registered bonds**—To be sold on U.S. markets, bonds must satisfy the stringent registration and disclosure requirements of the SEC.
- **Eurobonds**—Bonds denominated in U.S. dollars can be sold on the European exchanges, which have less stringent requirements.

Debt Covenants

Borrowers often must agree to obey restrictions, or debt covenants.

Positive covenants might include:

- Providing annual audited financial statements to the lender
- Maintaining minimum ratios of current assets to current liabilities or financial measures
- Maintaining life insurance policies on key officers or employees of the company

Negative covenants might include:

- Not borrowing additional sums during the time period from other lenders
- Not selling certain assets of the business
- Not paying dividends to shareholders
- Not exceeding certain compensation limits for executives

Bonds

Debt obligations may be secured by certain collateral or may specifically be placed behind other forms of debt in the priority of repayment. In roughly declining order of safety (and increasing order of interest rate), there are:

- **Mortgage bonds**—Secured by certain real estate owned by the borrower
- **Collateral trust bonds**—Secured by financial assets of the firm
- **Debentures**—Unsecured bonds
- **Subordinated debentures**—Unsecured bonds that will be repaid after all other creditors in the event of a liquidation of the corporation
- **Income bonds**—Bonds whose interest payments will be made only out of earnings of the corporation

Provisions Affecting Repayment of Bonds

The repayment of bonds may be affected by various provisions:

- **Term bonds**—Principal will be repaid on a single maturity date.
- **Serial bonds**—Principal repayment will occur in installments.
- **Sinking funds**—Regular deposits will be made by the borrower into an account from which repayment of the bonds will be made.
- **Convertible bonds**—The bondholder may convert the bonds to the common stock of the company as a form of repayment instead of holding them to maturity for cash.
- **Redeemable bonds**—The bondholder may be able to demand repayment of the bonds in advance of the normal maturity date should certain events occur (such as the buyout of the company by another firm).
- **Callable bonds**—The borrowing firm may force the bondholders to redeem the bonds before their normal maturity date (usually there is a set premium above the normal redemption price to compensate them for this forced liquidation).

Bond Interest Rates

There are three interest rates relevant to bonds:

1. **Stated rate**—The fixed interest payment calculated from the face value of the bond. It is also known as the **coupon rate, face rate,** or **nominal rate.**

2. **Current yield**—The fixed interest payment divided by the current selling price of the bond. When the bond is trading at a discount, this rate will be higher than the stated rate, and when the bond is trading at a premium, this rate will be lower than the stated rate. This rate can be somewhat misleading, since it reports the interest payment as a percentage of the current price but doesn't take into account the fact that the principal repayment of the bond will not be the current selling price but the face value.

3. **Yield to maturity**—The interest rate at which the present value of the cash flows of interest and principal will equal the current selling price of the bonds. For a bond selling at a discount, it will be even higher than the current yield, since it accounts for the "bonus" interest payment reflected in the discount. For a bond selling at a premium, this rate will be even lower than the current yield, since it reflects the loss of the premium when the principal is repaid. This rate is also known as the **effective rate** or **market rate.**

Variations on Bond Interest

Zero-coupon bond—This bond makes no interest payments at all and only pays the face value on the date of maturity. Short-term U.S. Treasury bills are a common example. A zero-coupon bond will always sell at a discount, since the interest is represented entirely by the difference between the price at which it is bought and the face value paid at maturity.

Floating rate bond—The interest payment is not fixed but fluctuates with some general index of interest rates. A **reverse floater** actually pays more interest when the general index goes down and less interest when the index goes up. Such an unusual bond might be used to hedge against the risk associated with floating rate bonds that the firm has issued.

Registered bond—The bondholder's name is registered with the firm, and interest payments are sent directly to the registered owner. In such cases, an actual bond certificate usually will not be issued.

Junk bond—This bond pays much higher than normal interest, since it was issued by a firm that has a poor credit rating and is more likely to default on its obligations. Bonds with a credit rating by Moody's Investors Service lower than Baa are usually considered junk bonds.

Foreign bond—This simply refers to a bond in which interest and principal is paid in another currency.

Preferred Stock

Preferred stock shareholders receive a stipulated dividend and priority over common shareholders in the event of liquidation of the business. Additional features preferred stock may include:

- **Cumulative dividends**—If stipulated dividends are not declared in a particular year, the amount becomes dividends in arrears and must be paid in later years before the common shareholders can receive any distribution.
- **Redeemability**—The shareholders may demand repayment of the face value at a specific date. In some cases, redemption is automatic. Such shares more closely resemble debt and are often presented before equity in the balance sheet.
- **Callability**—The firm may force the shareholders to redeem the shares.
- **Convertibility**—Shareholders can convert these shares to common stock.
- **Participation**—Preferred shareholders will receive a dividend that is higher than the stipulated rate when the common shareholders receive a higher rate.
- **Floating rate**—The dividend is variable based on some interest or inflation index.

Common Stock

Common stock shareholders are entitled to the residual (or leftover) assets and income after all creditors and preferred shareholders are paid.

Advantages to firm:

- The firm has no specific obligation to pay investors, increasing financial flexibility.
- Increased equity reduces the risk to lenders and reduces borrowing costs.

Disadvantages to firm:

- Issuance costs are greater than for debt.
- Ownership and control must be shared with all the new shareholders.
- Dividends are not tax-deductible.
- Shareholders ultimately receive a much higher return than lenders if the business is successful, so the long-run cost of capital obtained this way is typically much higher.

Introduction to Working Capital Management

Inventory conversion period (ICP) or inventory conversion cycle (ICC)—The average number of days required to convert inventory to sales

- ICP (ICC) = Average inventory / Cost of sales per day
- Average inventory = (Beginning inventory + Ending inventory) / 2
- Assume 365 days in a year unless told otherwise

Accounts receivable cycle (ARC)—The average number of days required to collect accounts receivable

- ARC = Average receivables / Credit sales per day

Accounts payable cycle (APC)—The average number of days between the purchase of inventory (including materials and labor for a manufacturing entity) on account and payment for them

- APC = Average payables / Purchases per day

Cash conversion cycle (CCC)—The average number of days between the payment of cash to suppliers of material and labor and cash inflows from customers

- CCC = ICP + ARC − APC

Cash Management

Cash balances are maintained by a firm for:

- **Operations**—To pay ordinary expenses
- **Compensating balances**—To receive various bank services, fee waivers, and loans
- **Trade discounts**—Quick payment of bills for early payment discounts
- **Speculative balances**—Funds to take advantage of special business opportunities
- **Precautionary balances**—Amounts that may be needed in emergency situations

Float refers to the time it takes for checks to be mailed, processed, and reflected in accounts. Management techniques try to maximize float on payments and minimize it on receipts.

- **Zero-balance accounts**—The firm is notified each day of checks presented for payment and transfers only the funds needed to cover them.
- **Lockbox system**—Customers send payments directly to bank to speed up deposits.
- **Concentration banking**—Customers pay to local branches instead of main offices.
- **Electronic funds transfers**—Customers pay electronically for fastest processing.

Focus on
Financial Management

Short-Term Securities Management

To maximize earnings on free cash, a firm may utilize various investments. Investments that are available through the federal government include:

- **Treasury bills**—Short-term obligations backed by the United States with original lives under 1 year that can be bought and sold easily from issuance to maturity date. These are in zero-coupon form and pay no formal interest, so they trade at a discount to maturity value.
- **Treasury notes**—Obligations with initial lives between 1 to 10 years. Formal interest payments are made semiannually.
- **Treasury bonds**—Same as notes but with original lives over 10 years.
- **Treasury Inflation-Protected Securities (TIPS)**—Treasury notes and bonds that pay a fixed rate of interest but with principal adjusted semiannually for inflation.
- **Federal agency securities**—Offerings that may or may not be backed by the full faith and credit of the United States and don't trade as actively as Treasuries but pay slightly higher rates.

Short-Term Securities Management (continued)

Other possible investments with free cash include:

- **Certificates of deposit**—Time deposits at banks that have limited government insurance.
- **Commercial paper**—Promissory notes from corporations with lives up to 9 months.
- **Banker's acceptance**—A draft drawn on a bank but payable at a specific future date (not on demand, as checks would be), usually 30 to 90 days after being drawn. These are usually generated by corporations to pay for goods, and may trade in secondary markets prior to the due date for payment at a discount.
- **Money market fund**—Shares in a mutual fund that invests in instruments with an average maturity date under 90 days, and which generally maintains a stable value for investors.
- **Short-term bond fund**—Shares in a mutual fund that invests in instruments with an average life over 90 days but under 5 years, generating higher returns than a money market fund but with some fluctuation in the principal value of the fund.
- **Equity and debt securities**—Individual stocks and bonds with substantially higher potential returns but also greater risk, including the risk of default. Should consider purchasing credit default insurance.

Accounts Receivable Management

A company sets credit policies for the granting and monitoring of receivables, including:

- **Credit period**—The time allowed for payment (typically 30 days)
- **Discounts**—Percentage reduction for early payment (such as 2% for payment in 10 days)
- **Credit criteria**—Financial strength requirements for customer to be granted credit
- **Collection policy**—Methods used to collect slow-paying accounts

In utilizing receivables to generate immediate cash, a firm's receivables may be:

- **Pledged**—A loan is obtained with the receivables offered as collateral for the loan.
- **Factored**—The receivables are actually sold to a financing company, which accepts the risk of noncollection and charges a percentage fee for accepting that risk (based on an estimate of the uncollectibles rate) as well as an interest rate based on the funds advanced prior to the date collection of the receivables is due.

Quality and Inventory Management

Economic Order Quantity (EOQ)

Minimizes total of order cost and carrying cost:

- **Order cost**—Cost of placing an order or starting a production run
- **Carrying cost**—Cost of having inventory on hand

$$EOQ = \sqrt{2AP/S}$$

A = Annual demand in units
P = Cost of placing an order or beginning a production run
S = Cost of carrying one unit in inventory for one period

Reorder Point and Safety Stock

Reorder point

- Units in inventory when order should be placed
- Average daily demand × Average lead time = Reorder point

Safety stock

- Extra units in inventory when placing order in case demand or lead time is greater than average
- Avoids costs associated with running out of stock
- Maximum daily demand × Maximum lead time – Reorder point = Safety stock

Just-in-Time (JIT) Purchasing

Costs reduced through:

- Reduction in inventory quantities
- Elimination of non-value-adding operations
- Most appropriate when order cost low and carrying cost high

Requires high-quality control standards

- Efficient system minimizing defective units
- Corrections made as defects occur
- Fewer vendors and suppliers

Just-in-Time (JIT) Purchasing (continued)

Problems of JIT system:

- Difficult to find suppliers able to accommodate
- High shipping costs due to smaller orders
- Potential problems due to delays in deliveries

May use backflush approach

- All manufacturing costs charged to cost of goods sold (COGS)
- Costs allocated from COGS to inventories at reporting dates

Quality Control

ISO Quality Standards—A series of standards established by the International Organization of Standards.

- **ISO 9000 Series**—Standards consisting of five parts (9000 to 9004) that focus on the quality of products and services provided by firms
- **ISO 14000 Series**—Standards focused on pollution reduction and other environmental goals

Pareto Principle—An attempt to focus on the small number of significant quality issues, based on an estimate that 80% of all problems come from only 20% of all causes.

Six Sigma Quality—A statistical measure of the percentage of products that are in acceptable form, based on standard deviation measures. One sigma means that approximately 68% of products are acceptable. Six sigmas would indicate 99.999997% of products meet quality standards, and constitute a hypothetical goal of perfection in manufacturing.

Kaizen—Japanese art of continuous improvement. This theory emphasizes identification by all members of a company of small potential improvements rather than searching for big breakthroughs.

Delphi—Separate consultation with multiple experts and tabulation of recommendations.

Cost of Quality

The costs related to quality rise the later in the process the firm deals with it. There are four different stages at which costs can be addressed:

1. **Prevention costs**—Prevent product failure

   - Use high-quality materials
   - Inspect production process
   - Train employees
   - Maintain machines

2. **Appraisal or detection costs**—Detect product failure before production is complete

   - Inspect samples of finished goods
   - Obtain information from customers

Cost of Quality (continued)

3. **Internal failure costs**—Detect product failure after production but before shipment to customer

    - Scrap resulting from wasted materials
    - Reworking units to correct defects
    - Reinspection and retesting after rework

4. **External failure costs**—Defective product sent to customer

    - Warranty costs
    - Dealing with customer complaints
    - Product liability
    - Marketing to improve image
    - Lost sales

Liquidity Measures

Current Ratio = Current assets / Current liabilities

Quick (or Acid Test) Ratio = Quick assets / Current liabilities

- **Quick assets** = Cash + Marketable securities + Accounts receivable

Operational Activity Measures

Receivable Turnover = Net credit sales / Average accounts receivable

- **Average accounts receivable (A/R)** = (Beginning A/R + Ending A/R) / 2
- Remember to use net credit sales, **not** net sales

Receivables Collection Period = Average accounts receivable / Average credit sales per day

- Use 365-day year unless told otherwise

Inventory Turnover = Cost of goods sold / Average inventory

- Remember to use cost of goods sold, **not** sales

Inventory Conversion Period = Average inventory / Average cost of goods sold per day

Fixed Asset Turnover = Sales / Average net fixed assets

- Remember that net fixed assets is after subtraction of accumulated depreciation

Total Asset Turnover = Sales / Average total assets

Profitability Measures

Gross Margin = Gross profit / Net sales

Gross Profit = Sales revenue – Cost of goods sold

Operating Profit Margin = Operating profit / Net sales

Return on Assets = [Net income + (add back) Interest expense (net of tax effect)] / Average total assets

- **Average Total Assets** = (Beginning total assets + Ending total assets) / 2

Return on Equity = Net income / Average stockholders' equity

- **Average Stockholders' Equity** = (Beginning total stockholders' equity + Ending total stockholders' equity) / 2

Return on Common Stockholders' Equity = [Net income – Preferred dividend (obligation for the period only)] / Average common stockholders' equity

- **Average Common Stockholders' Equity** = (Beginning common stockholders' equity + Ending common stockholders' equity) / 2

Equity/Investment Leverage Measure

Debt to Total Assets = Total liabilities / Total assets

Debt to Equity Ratio = Total debt / Total equity

Times Interest Earned Ratio = Earnings before interest and taxes / Interest expense

PERFORMANCE MEASURES AND MANAGEMENT TECHNIQUES

Manufacturing Costs

Cost Classifications

Product and Period Costs

	Product	Period
Direct materials (DM)	x	
Direct labor (DL)	x	
Manufacturing overhead (MOH)	x	
Selling, general, and administrative expenses (SG&A)		x

Cost Classifications (continued)

Prime and Conversion Costs

	Prime	Conversion
DM	x	
DL	x	x
MOH		x

Variable and Fixed Costs

	Variable	Fixed
DM	x	
DL	x	
MOH	x	x
SG&A	x	x

Costing Methods

DM used
+ DL incurred
+ MOH applied
→ Work-in-process inventory (WIP)

Cost of complete units

Finished goods

Cost of units sold

Cost of good sold

Manufacturing Overhead

1. Calculate the predetermined overhead rate (POHR)

> **Estimated variable MOH for period**
+ Estimated fixed MOH for period
= Estimated total MOH for period
÷ Estimated # of units for period (cost driver)
= Predetermined overhead rate (POHR)—often split into fixed and variable rates

2. Apply MOH to WIP

> Actual # of units for period (cost driver)
× POHR
= MOH Applied

Manufacturing Overhead (continued)

3. Determine under-applied or over-applied MOH
   - Actual MOH > MOH applied: MOH under-applied
   - Actual MOH < MOH applied: MOH over-applied
4. Dispose of under-applied or over-applied MOH
   - Generally added to or deducted from cost of good sold (COGS)
   - May be charged or credited directly to income
   - May be allocated to WIP, finished goods, and COGS

Spoilage, Cost, and Inventory Flows

Different types of unused units or materials have different accounting treatments:

Normal spoilage—Product cost (added to cost of good units)

Abnormal spoilage—Period cost (charged against income in period)

Scrap—Generally charged to cost of goods manufactured

Proceeds from sale of scrap:

- Additional income
- Reduce cost of sales
- Reduce manufacturing overhead
- Reduce cost of specific job

Cost Behavior Patterns

Calculating Total Costs

Total costs = Fixed costs + Variable costs

$$y = a + bx$$

y = Total cost (dependent variable)

a = Total fixed costs

b = Variable cost per unit

x = # of units (independent variable)

Various methods are used to determine the variable cost per unit and total fixed costs

Cost Drivers

Units represent volume of cost driver

- Cost driver can be any variable that has greatest influence on cost
- Examples include volume of production, hours worked, miles driven, or machine hours

High-Low Method

Four steps in estimating variable cost per unit and total fixed costs

1. | Highest volume | Total cost | # of units |
   |---|---|---|
   | Lowest volume | Total cost | # of units |
   | Difference | Cost | # of units |

2. Variable cost per unit = Difference in cost ÷ Difference in # of units
3. Total variable costs (at either level) = Variable cost per unit × # of units
4. Fixed costs (at either level) = Total costs – Total variable costs

Regression Analysis

Coefficient of correlation (R) indicates relationship between dependent and independent variable:

- R = 1 — Strong direct relationship
- 1 > R > 0 — Direct relationship, not as strong
- R = 0 — No relationship
- 0 > R > −1 — Indirect relationship, not as strong
- R = −1 — Strong indirect relationship

Company will use cost driver with strongest direct or indirect relationship

Activity-Based Costing and Process Management

Method of analyzing and reducing MOH

- MOH segregated into pools
- Cost driver identified for each pool
- MOH applied using multiple rates

Identifies costs that are nonvalue adding

- Can be used to reduce overhead
- Identify and minimize nonvalue adding costs

Also used to allocate service department costs

Under step allocation method

- Service departments allocated beginning with those serving most other departments
- Allocation based on that department's cost driver
- Costs allocated to all remaining service departments and production departments
- Costs not charged back to service departments already allocated
- Process complete when only production departments remain

Activity-Based Costing and Process Management (continued)

		Service departments				Production departments	
		#1	#2	#3	#4	#1	#2
Costs		$	$	$	$	$	$
	Allocation	($)	$	$	$	$	$
Subtotal		0	$	$	$	$	$
	Allocation		($)	$	$	$	$
Subtotal			0	$	$	$	$
	Allocation			($)	$	$	$
Subtotal				0	$	$	$
	Allocation				($)	$	$
Total					0	$	$

Absorption and Direct Costing

Absorption Costing

- Used for financial statements
- Inventory includes DM + DL + Variable MOH + Fixed MOH

Variable Costing

- Used for internal purposes only
- Inventory includes DM + DL + Variable MOH

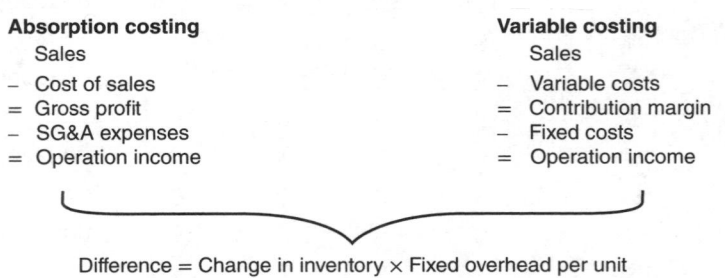

Absorption costing
  Sales
- Cost of sales
= Gross profit
- SG&A expenses
= Operation income

Variable costing
  Sales
- Variable costs
= Contribution margin
- Fixed costs
= Operation income

Difference = Change in inventory × Fixed overhead per unit

Job Order Costing and Overhead Allocation

Used when units are relatively expensive and costs can be identified to units or batches

- DM, DL, and MOH applied charged to WIP
- Cost of completed units removed from WIP and charged to finished goods
- Cost of units sold removed from finished goods and charged to COGS

Process Costing

Used when units are relatively inexpensive and costs cannot be identified to units or batches

- DM, DL, and MOH applied charged to WIP
- Calculates average cost of equivalent units produced during period
- Average costs used to transfer from WIP to finished goods and from finished goods to COGS

Calculating equivalent units

- Costs incurred at beginning of process—Equivalent units = Units × 100%
- Costs incurred at end of process—Equivalent units = Units × 0%
- Costs incurred uniformly—Equivalent units = Units × % complete
- Costs incurred at particular point
    - If units reached that point—Equivalent units = Units × 100%
    - If units haven't reached that point—Equivalent units = Units × 0%

Process Costing (continued)

Process costing—**weighted-average**

1.   Costs in beginning WIP
   + Costs incurred during period
   = Total costs to be allocated

2.   Units completed during period
   + Equivalent units in ending WIP
   = Total equivalent production

3.   Total costs to be allocated
   ÷ Total equivalent production
   = Average cost per equivalent unit

4.   Units completed during period
   × Average cost per equivalent unit
   = Amount allocated to finished goods

5.   Equivalent units in ending inventory
   × Average cost per equivalent unit
   = Amount allocated to ending WIP

Process Costing (continued)

Process costing—**FIFO**

1.   Determine costs incurred during period

2.   Units in beginning WIP
   - Equivalent units in beginning WIP
   = Equivalent units required to complete beginning WIP

3.   Equivalent units required to complete beginning WIP
   ÷ Units started and completed during period × 100%
   + Equivalent units in ending WIP
   = Total equivalent production

Process Costing (continued)

4.   Costs incurred during period

    ÷ Total equivalent production

    = Average cost per equivalent unit

5.   Costs in beginning WIP

    + Units started and completed × Average cost per equivalent unit

    = Amount allocated to finished goods

6.   Equivalent units in ending WIP

    × Average cost per equivalent unit

    = Amount allocated to ending WIP

Joint and By-Product Costing

Joint Product Costing

Joint products—two or more products resulting from same process

- **Joint product costs**—costs incurred before products separated
- **Split-off point**—earliest point at which products can be separated
- **Sales value**—amount each product can be sold for at earliest point of sale
- **Separable costs**—costs incurred after split-off point before products can be sold
- **Relative sales value**—Sales value—Separable costs

Joint Product Costing (continued)

Allocating joint product costs—relative sales value method

1. Calculate relative sales value for each joint product
2. Add together to calculate total relative sales value
3. Calculate ratio of relative sales value for each joint product to total relative sales value
4. Multiply ratio for each product by joint product costs
5. Result is amount of joint product costs to be allocated to each product

Accounting for By-Products

Revenues from sale of by-products generally reduce cost of other products

1. Determine revenues from sale of by-products
2. Reduce by separable costs, if any, and costs of disposal
3. Net amount reduces cost of primary product or joint costs

Budgeting

Used to estimate revenue, costs, a group of costs, or profits at various levels of activity

- Applies when operating within a relevant range
- Total fixed costs remain the same at all levels within range
- Variable costs per unit of activity remains the same within range

Master and Static Budgets

Static budget—Budget as specific level of activity

- Can be for division of company
- Can be for company as a whole

Master budget—Static budget for company as a whole

Master budget generally includes:

- Operating budget
- Budgeted cash flows
- Budgeted financial statements

Preparing a Master Budget

1. Estimate sales volume
2. Use sales volume to estimate revenues
3. Use collection history to estimate collections
4. Estimate cost of sales based on units sold
5. Use current finished goods inventory, budgeted ending inventory, and cost of sales to estimate units to be manufactured
6. Use units manufactured to estimate material needs, labor costs, and overhead costs
7. Use material needs, current raw materials inventory, and budgeted ending inventory to budget purchases
8. Use purchase terms to estimate payments
9. Analyze expense and payment patterns to complete operating and cash flow budgets

Budgeting Material Purchases and Payments

	Units sold
+	Budgeted increase in finished goods
−	Budgeted decrease in finished goods
=	Units to be manufactured
×	Units of raw material per unit of finished goods
=	Units of raw material required for production
+	Budgeted increase in raw materials
−	Budgeted decrease in raw materials
=	**Budgeted raw material purchases**
+	Budgeted decrease in accounts payable
−	Budgeted increase in accounts payable
=	**Budgeted payments for raw materials**

Sales and Direct Cost Variance

Material Variances

Standard cost (Units produced × Std qty per unit × Std cost per unit)
- − Actual material cost
- = Total material variance

Material price variance (MPV)
- + Material usage variance (MUV)
- = Total material variance

MPV = Act qty × (Std pr − Act pr)   MUV = Std pr × (Std qty − Act qty)

Sales and Direct Cost Variance (continued)

Labor Variances

Standard cost (Units produced × Std hrs per unit × Std rate per hr)
 − Actual labor cost
 = Total labor variance

              Labor rate variance (LRV)
+ Labor efficiency variance (LEV)
= Total labor variance

LRV = Act qty × (Std rate − Act rate)   LEV = Std rate × (Std hrs − Act hrs)

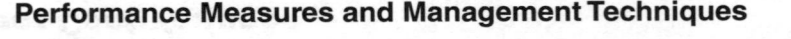

Overhead Variance Analysis

Overhead Variances

Overhead applied (Std hrs × Total POHR)
– Actual overhead cost
= Total overhead variance

    Overhead volume variance (OVV)
+ Overhead efficiency variance (OEV)
+ Overhead spending variance (OSV)
= Total overhead variance

Std hrs × POHR (fixed)	Std hrs × POHR (Variance)	Act hrs × POHR (total)
– Budgeted fixed OH	– Act hrs × POHR (Variance)	+ Budgeted fixed OH
= OVV	= OEV	– Act OH
		= OSV

Forecasting Techniques

Sensitivity analysis used to evaluate results of decisions under various conditions

Probability Analysis

Long-term average result (expected value) of decision is estimated

1. Each possible outcome of decision is assigned a probability
2. Total of probabilities is 100%
3. Profit or loss under each possible outcome is determined
4. Profit or loss for outcome multiplied by probability
5. Total of results is added
6. Result is long-term average result

Relevant Costs 1 & 2

Increase or decrease in profits or costs resulting from decision is analyzed

1. Determine increase or decrease in revenues that will result from decision
2. Determine increase or decrease in variable costs that will result from decision
3. Determine if decision will affect fixed costs
4. Net of change in revenues, variable costs, and fixed costs is relevant cost of making decision

Lease versus Buy: Compare Both Options Using Discounted Cash Flow

1. Leasing may require lower initial investment
2. Operating leases off balance sheet
3. Capital leases shift risk of ownership from lessor to lessee

Regression Analysis

Coefficient of correlation (R) indicates relationship between dependent and independent variable:

- $R = 1$ Strong direct relationship
- $1 > R > 0$ Direct relationship, not as strong
- $R = 0$ No relationship
- $0 > R > -1$ Indirect relationship, not as strong
- $R = -1$ Strong indirect relationship

Company will use cost driver with strongest direct or indirect relationship

Cost-Volume-Profit Analysis Calculations

    Sales price per unit   Contrib margin per unit
− Variable cost per unit   ÷ Sales price per unit
= Contrib margin per unit   = Contrib margin ratio

Units   **Dollars**

Breakeven

    Fixed costs   Fixed costs
÷ Contrib margin per unit   ÷ Contrib margin ratio
= Breakeven in units   = Breakeven in dollars

Profit as fixed amount

    Fixed costs + Desired profit   Fixed costs + Desired profit
÷ Contrib margin per unit   ÷ Contrib margin ratio
= Units required to earn desired profit   = Sales dollars required to earn desired profit

Profit as percentage of sales

    Fixed costs   Fixed costs
÷ Contrib margin − Profit per unit   ÷ (Contrib margin − Profit) ÷ Sales price
= Units required to earn profit ratio   =   Sales required to earn profit ratio

Graphical Approach to Breakeven

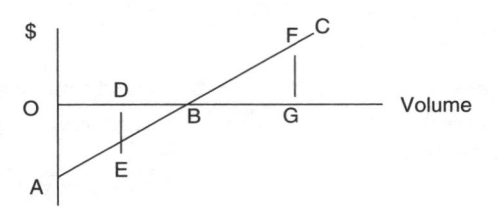

AC	= Profit for product at various levels of production
B	= Breakeven point
OA	= Fixed costs
DE	= Loss at production point D (below breakeven)
FG	= Profit at production point G (above breakeven)
OA ÷ OB	= Contribution margin
FG ÷ BG	= Contribution margin

Transfer Pricing and Benchmarking

Transfer price—price at which products are transferred from one department to another within the same company

Possible transfer prices:

- Actual cost
- Market value
- Cost + profit
- Negotiated amount
- Standard cost

Transfer from cost center to profit center—generally use standard variable cost

- Cost center evaluated based on comparing standard variable cost to actual cost
- Profit center not affected by performance of cost center

Measurement Frameworks

Balanced scorecards attempt to translate an organization's goals into specific measures with four perspectives:

1. **Financial**—Return on investment and related financial measures
2. **Customer**—Nonfinancial measures of customer satisfaction and retention
3. **Internal business processes**—Measures of operating effectiveness and efficiency including financial measures, such as cost variances, and nonfinancial measures, such as number of defects in production
4. **Learning and growth**—Measures of employee satisfaction, training, and advancement

Value-based management examines all aspects of a company with the intention of identifying the amount of **economic value added (EVA)** by different activities. In effect, it attempts to translate all activities into their financial value to the firm, and is comparable to a financial scorecard focus.

Balanced Scorecard and Benchmarking

The components of a balanced scorecard include:

- **Strategic objectives**—A statement of the goals of the firm and necessary elements
- **Performance measures**—Identification of quantitative methods that can be used to track success in fulfilling the strategic objectives
- **Baseline performance**—The current level of performance for each measure
- **Targets**—The level or improvement in performance being sought
- **Strategic initiatives**—Programs that will help achieve the targets and objectives

Cause-and-effect linkages identify which performance measures are **performance drivers** (leading indicators) and which are **outcome performance measures** (lagging indicators). This allows the firm to focus on those drivers that are critical to strategic objectives.

Strategy maps are diagrams that identify cause-and-effect linkages:

Value-Based Management

Return on Investment (based on assets) = Net income / Total assets

DuPont return on investment (ROI) analysis: ROI = Return on sales × Asset turnover

- **Return on sales** = Net income / Sales
- **Asset turnover** = Sales / Total assets

Residual income = Operating profit – Interest on investment

- **Interest on investment** = Invested capital × Required rate of return

Economic Value Added: EVA = Net operating profit after taxes (NOPAT) – Cost of financing

- **Cost of financing** = (Total assets – Current liabilities) × Weighted-average cost of capital

Free Cash Flow = NOPAT + Depreciation + Amortization – Capital expenditures – Net increase in working capital

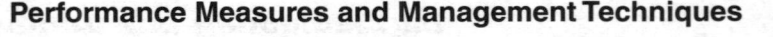

Business Process Management: Focus on Continuous Improvement in Processes to Meet Customers' Needs

Business Processes: Assets in Themselves

1. Design: Identify existing processes/possible improvements
2. Modeling: What-if analyses
3. Execution
   a. Install new software
   b. Test
   c. Train employees
   d. Implement new processes
4. Monitor with performance statistics
5. Optimize
   a. Use performance statistics to identify bottlenecks
   b. Consider strategies (e.g., outsourcing) to remove bottlenecks

Business Process Management: Focus on Continuous Improvement in Processes to Meet Customers' Needs *(continued)*

6. Other techniques

   a. Reengineer

   b. Lean manufacturing (shorten time by eliminating waste)

   c. Theory of constraints: Increase throughput contribution margin by decreasing investment and operating costs. Must identify and remediate:

      1) Bottleneck resources: capacity is less than demand

      2) Non-bottleneck resources: capacity greater than demand

7. Workflow analysis: Focus on eliminating non-value-added activities

Project Management and Benchmarking

A project is a series of activities and tasks that

- Have specific definable objectives
- Have defined start and end dates
- Are subject to funding constraints
- Consume resources, people, equipment, etc.
- Cut across various functional areas of the organization

Effective project management: Four basic elements

1. Resources
2. Time
3. Money
4. Scope

Project Management and Benchmarking (continued)

Effective project management: Five processes/cycles

1. Project initiation
   a. Support of management
   b. Project manager with authority
   c. Project charter

2. Project planning
   a. Define scope
   b. Identify resources needed
   c. Schedule tasks
   d. Identify risks

Project Management and Benchmarking (continued)

3. Project execution
   a. Managing work
   b. Directing team
4. Project monitoring and control
   a. Tracking progress
   b. Comparing actual outcomes to predicted outcomes (variances)
5. Project closure

Project Management Tools

1. Life-cycle approach: Define and assess each phase of project
2. Gantt chart—bar chart that illustrates the scheduled start and finish of elements of a project over time

Project Management and Benchmarking (continued)

3. Program Evaluation and Review Technique (PERT): Focus on the interdependency of activities and the time required to complete an activity to schedule and control the project
   a. Critical path: The shortest amount of time necessary to accomplish the project.
      1) Optimistic
      2) Most likely
      3) Pessimistic
4. PERT used where there is a high variability of completion time, such as R&D
5. ABC analysis: Categorize tasks into three groups:
   a. Tasks that are perceived as being urgent and important
   b. Tasks that are important but not urgent
   c. Tasks that are neither urgent nor important

INDEX

Index